Fields of Gold

Music and lyrics by Sting
Arranged for harp by Sylvia Woods

This sheet music includes two arrangements playable on either lever or pedal harp. There are no lever or pedal changes required in either version.

The harp range needed for the Intermediate Arrangement (page 1) is 22 strings, or 3 octaves from C to C.

The easier Advanced Beginner Arrangement (page 5) needs 19 strings from F up to C.

If you have a small harp, you may need to play the music an octave higher than written.

Fields of Gold

Intermediate harp arrangement

Music and Lyrics by Sting
Harp Arrangement by Sylvia Woods

Whenever there are two descending notes going down to a chord, slide your right thumb from the first note to the second, and then slide to the top note of the chord. I have marked the first few. Play the rest in the same manner.

Flowing, moderately

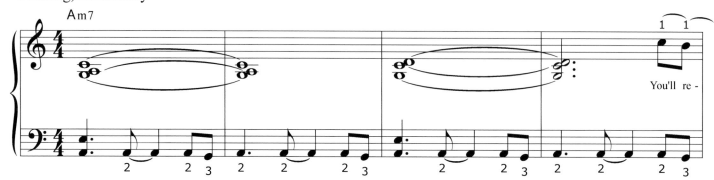

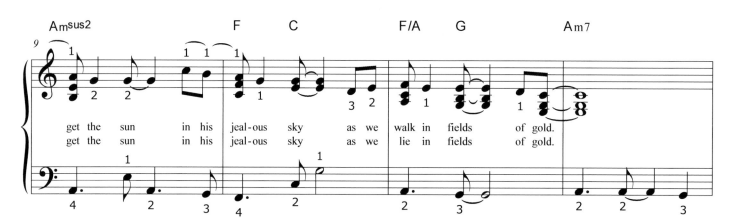

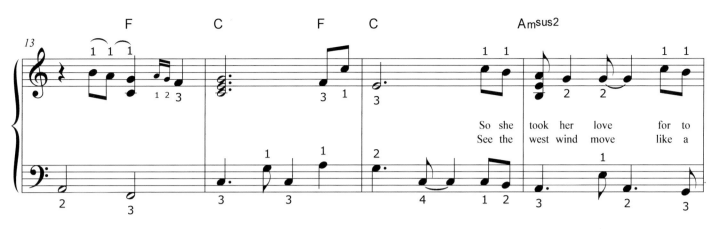

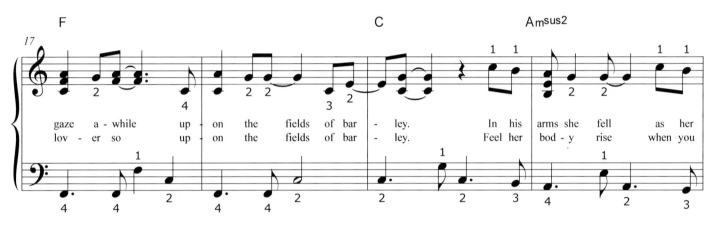

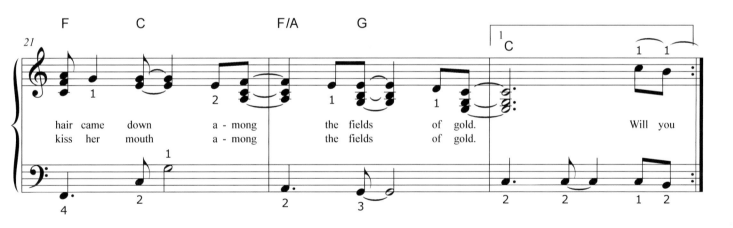

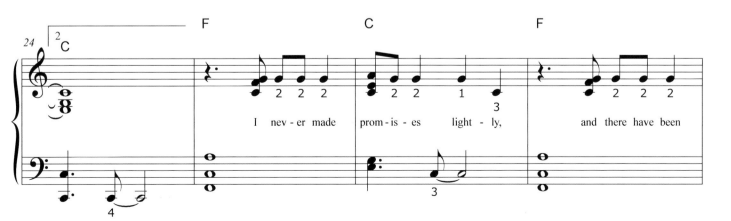

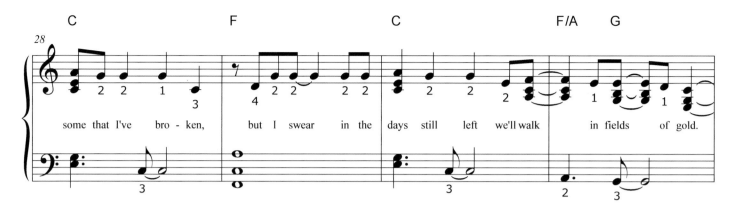

some that I've bro - ken,   but I swear   in the   days still   left we'll walk   in fields   of gold.

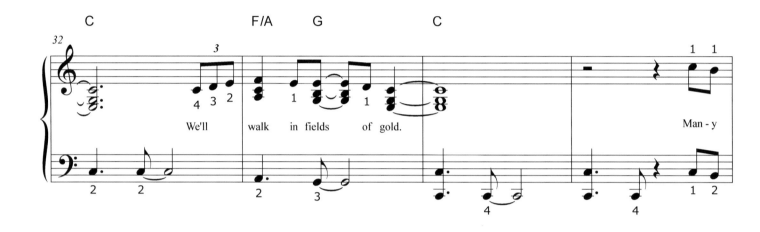

We'll   walk   in fields   of gold.   Man - y

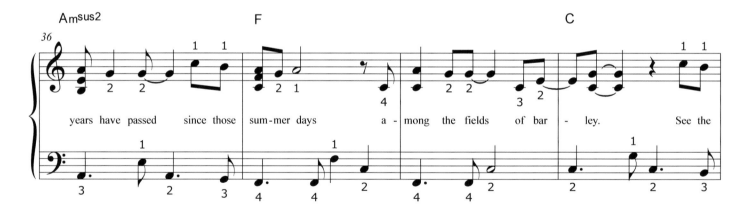

years have passed   since those   sum-mer days   a - mong the fields   of bar - ley.   See the

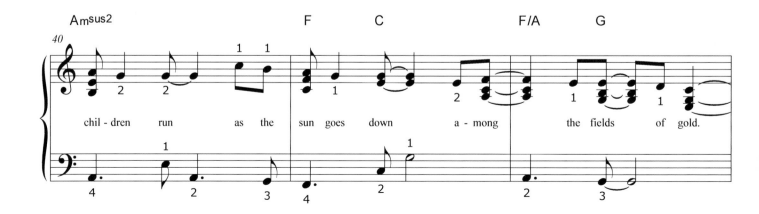

chil - dren   run   as the   sun goes   down   a - mong   the fields   of gold.

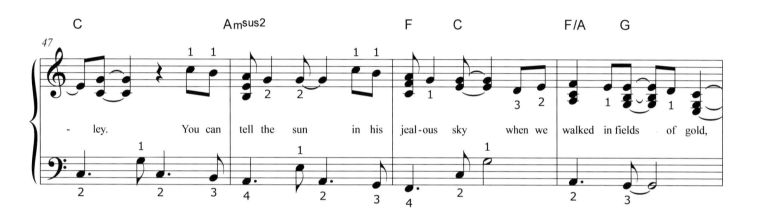

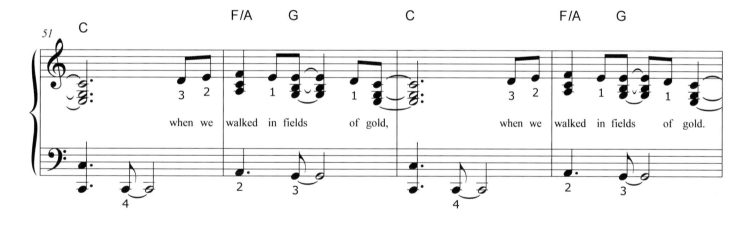

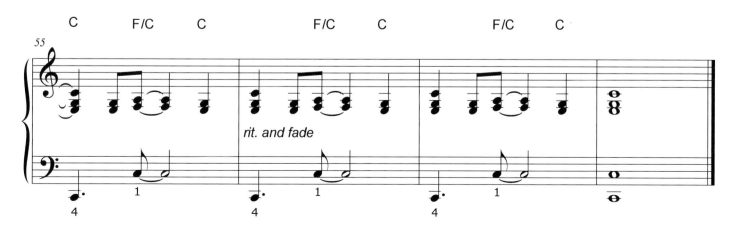

Fields of Gold

Advanced beginner harp arrangement

Music and Lyrics by Sting
Harp Arrangement by Sylvia Woods

Flowing, moderately

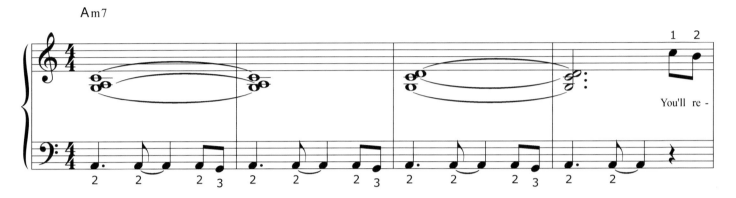

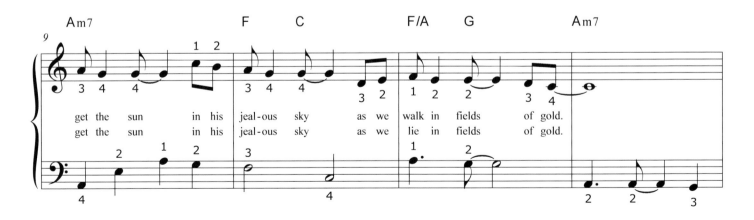

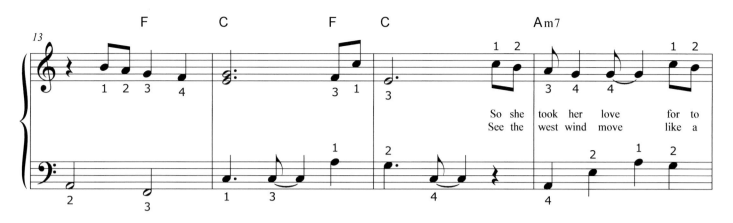

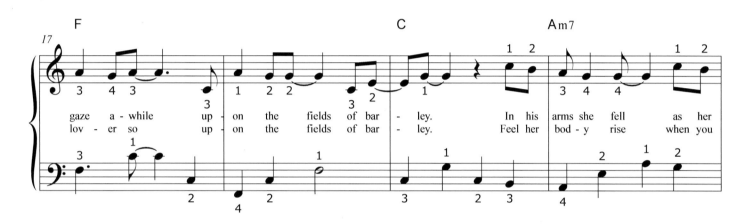

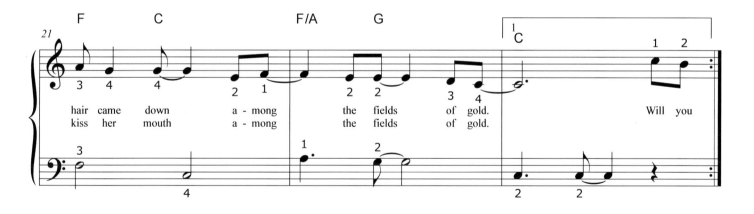

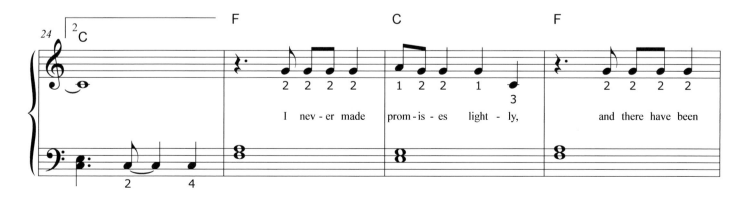

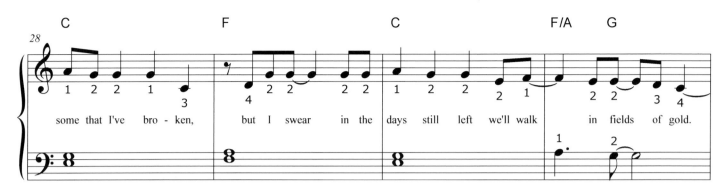

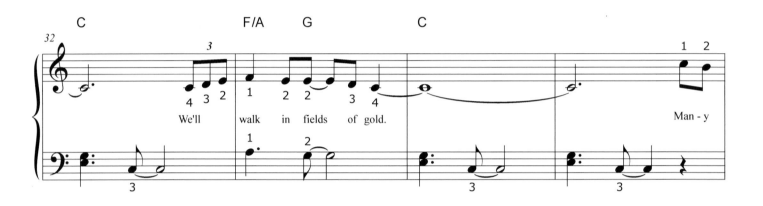

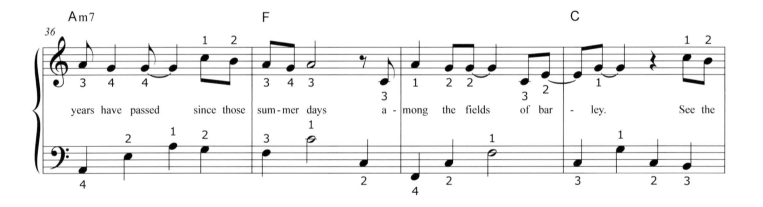

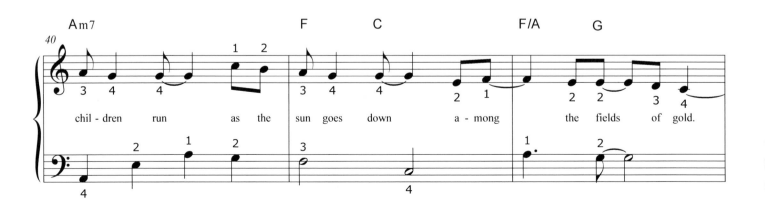